The Dogmas of Judaism

By

Anonymous

Published by Left of Brain Books

Copyright © 2023 Left of Brain Books

ISBN 978-1-397-66775-5

First Edition

All rights reserved. No part of this publication may be reproduced, distributed, or transmitted in any form or by any means, including photocopying, recording, or other electronic or mechanical methods, without the prior written permission of the publisher, except in the case of brief quotations permitted by copyright law. Left of Brain Books is a division of Left Of Brain Onboarding Pty Ltd.

PUBLISHER'S PREFACE

About the Book

"Judaism is the religion of the Jewish people, based on principles and ethics embodied in the Hebrew Bible (Tanakh), as further explored and explained in the Talmud. In 2007, the world Jewish population was estimated at 13.2 million people- 41 percent in Israel and 59 in the diaspora.

According to Jewish tradition, the history of Judaism begins with the Covenant between God and Abraham (ca. 2000 [BC]), the patriarch and progenitor of the Jewish people. Judaism is among the oldest religious traditions still in practice today. Jewish history and doctrines have influenced other religions such as Christianity, Islam and the Baha'i Faith.

Judaism differs from many religions in that in modern times, central authority is not vested in any single person or group, but in sacred texts, traditions, and learned Rabbis who interpret those texts and laws. Throughout the ages, Judaism has clung to a number of religious principles, the most important of which is the belief in a single, omniscient, omnipotent, benevolent, transcendent God, who created the universe and continues to govern it. According to traditional Jewish belief, the God who created the world established a covenant with the Israelites, and revealed his laws and commandments to Moses on Mount Sinai in the form of the Torah, and the Jewish people are the descendants of the Israelites. The traditional practice of Judaism revolves around study and the observance of God's laws and commandments as written in the Torah and expounded in the Talmud."

(Quote from wikipedia.org)

CONTENTS

PUBLISHER'S PREFACE
INTRODUCTORY MATERIAL 1
    THE BIBLE: ARE WE COMMANDED TO BELIEVE? 6
    THE MISHNAH - SANHEDRIN AS SOURCE FOR DOGMA 11
    CARAITE BELIEF 14
    SAADIAH AND THE BEGINNING OF JEWISH DOGMA 17
    MAIMONIDES AND THE 13 ARTICLES 19
    THE ANTI-MAIMONISTS 22
    CHASDAI IBN CRESCAS 26
    ALBO 31
    ABARBANEL 34
    DELMEDIGO 36

INTRODUCTORY MATERIAL

THE object of this essay is to say about the dogmas of Judaism a word which I think ought not to be left unsaid.

In speaking of dogmas it must be understood that Judaism does not ascribe to them any saving power. The belief in a dogma or a doctrine without abiding by its real or supposed consequences (eg. the, belief in creatio ex nihilo without keeping the Sabbath) is of no value. And the question about certain doctrines is not whether they possess or do not possess the desired charm against certain diseases of the soul, but whether they ought to be considered as characteristics of Judaism or not.

It must again be premised that the subject, which occupied the thoughts of the greatest and noblest Jewish minds for so many centuries, has been neglected for a comparatively long time. And this for various reasons. First, there is Mendelssohn's assertion, or supposed assertion, in his Jerusalem, that Judaism has no dogmas -- an assertion which has been accepted by the majority of modern Jewish theologians as the only dogma Judaism possesses. You can hear it pronounced in scores of Jewish pulpits; you can read it written in scores of Jewish books. To admit the possibility that Mendelssohn was in error was hardly permissible, especially for those with whom he enjoys a certain infallibility. Nay, even the fact that he himself was not consistent in his theory, and on another occasion declared that Judaism has dogmas, only that they are purer and more in harmony with reason than those of other religions; or even the more important fact that he published a school-book for children, in which the so-called Thirteen Articles were embodied, only that instead of the formula "I believe," he substituted "I am convinced," -- even such patent facts did not produce much effect upon many of our modern theologians. [n. 1] They were either overlooked or explained away so as to make them harmonise with the great dogma of dogmalessness. For it is one of the attributes of infallibility, that the words of its happy possessor must always be reconcilable even when they appear to the eye of the unbeliever as gross contradictions.

Another cause of the neglect into which the subject has fallen is that our century is an historical one. It is not only books that have their fate, but also whole sciences and literatures. In past times it was religious speculation that formed the favorite study of scholars, in our time it is history with its critical foundation on a sound philology. Now as these two most important branches of Jewish science were so long neglected -- were perhaps never cultivated in the true meaning of the word, and as Jewish literature is so vast and Jewish history so far-reaching and eventful, we cannot wonder that these studies have absorbed the time and the labour of the greatest and best Jewish writers in this century.

There is, besides, a certain tendency in historical studies that is hostile to mere theological speculation. The historian deals with realities, the theologian with abstractions. The latter likes to shape the universe after his system, and tells us how things ought to be, the former teaches us how they are or have been, and the explanation he gives for their being so and not otherwise includes in most cases also a kind of justification for their existence. There is also the odium theologicum, which has been the cause of so much misfortune that it is hated by the historian, whilst the superficial, rationalistic way in which the theologian manages to explain everything which does not suit his system is most repulsive to the critical spirit.

But it cannot be denied that this neglect has caused much confusion. Especially is this noticeable in England, which is essentially a theological country, and where people are but little prone to give up speculation about things which concern their most sacred interest and greatest happiness. Thus whilst we are exceedingly poor in all other branches of Jewish learning, we are comparatively rich in productions of a theological character. We have a superfluity of essays on such delicate subjects as eternal punishment, immortality of the soul, the day of judgment, etc., and many treatises on the definition of Judaism. But knowing little or nothing of the progress recently made in Jewish theology, of the many protests against all kinds of infallibility, whether canonised in this century or in olden times, we in England still maintain that Judaism has no dogmas as if nothing to the contrary had ever been said. We seek the foundation of Judaism in political economy, in hygiene, in everything except religion. Following the fashion of the day to esteem religion in proportion to its ability to adapt itself to every possible and impossible metaphysical and social system, we are anxious to squeeze out of Judaism the last drop of faith and hope, and strive to make it so flexible that we can turn it in every direction which it is our pleasure to follow. But alas! the flexibility has progressed so far as to classify Judaism among the invertebrate species, the lowest order of living things. It strongly resembles a certain Christian school which addresses itself to the world in general and claims to satisfy everybody alike. It claims to be socialism for the adherents of Karl Marx and Lassalle, worship of man for the followers of Comte and St. Simon; it carefully avoids the word "God" for the comfort of agnostics and sceptics, whilst on the other hand it pretends to hold sway over paradise, hell, and immortality for the edification of believers. In such illusions many of our theologians delight. For illusions they are; you cannot be everything if you want to be anything. Moreover, illusions in themselves are bad enough, but we are menaced with what is still worse. Judaism, divested of every higher religious motive, is in danger of falling into gross materialism. For what else is the meaning of such declarations as "Believe what you like, but conform to this or that mode of life"; what else does it mean but "We cannot expect you to believe that the things you are bidden to do are commanded by a higher authority; there is not such a thing as belief, but you ought to do them for conventionalism or for your own convenience."

But both these motives -- the good opinion of our neighbours, as well as our bodily health -- have nothing to do with our nobler and higher sentiments, and degrade Judaism to a matter of expediency or diplomacy. Indeed, things have advanced so far that well-meaning, but ill-advised writers even think to render a service to Judaism by declaring it to be a kind of enlightened Hedonism, or rather a moderate Epicureanism.

I have no intention of here answering the question, What is Judaism? This question is not less perplexing than the problem, What is God's world? Judaism is also a great Infinite, composed of as many endless Units, the Jews. And these Unit-Jews have been, and are still, scattered through all the world, and have passed under an immensity of influences, good and bad. If so, how can we give an exact definition of the Infinite, called Judaism?

But if there is anything sure, it is that the highest motives which worked through the history of Judaism are the strong belief in God and the unshaken confidence that at last this God, the God of Israel, will be the God of the whole world; or, in other words, Faith and Hope are the two most prominent characteristics of Judaism.

In the following pages I shall try to give a short account of the manner in which these two principles of Judaism found expression, from the earliest times down to the age of Mendelssohn; that is, to present an outline of the history of Jewish Dogmas. First, a few observations on the position of the Bible and the Talmud in relation to our theme. Insufficient and poor as they may be in proportion to the importance of these two fundamental documents of Judaism, these remarks may nevertheless suggest a connecting link between the teachings of Jewish antiquity and those of Maimonides and his successors.

THE BIBLE: ARE WE COMMANDED TO BELIEVE?

I begin with the Scriptures.

THE Bible itself hardly contains a command bidding us to believe. We are hardly ordered, e.g., to believe in the existence of God. I say hardly, but I do not altogether deny the existence of such a command. It is true that we do not find in the Scripture such words as: "You are commanded to believe in the existence of God." Nor is any punishment assigned as awaiting him who denies it. Notwithstanding these facts, many Jewish authorities -- among them such important men as Maimonides, R. Judah Hallevi, Nachmanides -- perceive, in the first words of the Ten Commandments, "I am the Lord thy God," the command to believe in His existence. [n. 2]

Be this as it may, there cannot be the shadow of a doubt that the Bible, in which every command is dictated by God, and in which all its heroes are the servants, the friends, or the ambassadors of God, presumes such a belief in every one to whom those laws are dictated, and these heroes address themselves. Nay, I think that the word "belief" is not even adequate. In a world with so many visible facts and invisible causes, as life and death, growth and decay, light and darkness; in a world where the sun rises and sets; where the stars appear regularly; where heavy rains pour down from the sky, often accompanied by such grand phenomena as thunder and lightning; in a world full of such marvels, but into which no notion has entered of all our modern true or false explanations -- who but God is behind all these things? "Have the gates," asks

God, "have the gates of death been open to thee? or hast thou seen the doors of the shadow of death? . . .Where is the way where light dwelleth? and as for darkness, where is the place thereof ? . . . Hath the rain a father? or who hath begotten the drops of dew? . . . Canst thou bind the sweet influences of Pleiades, or loose the bands of Orion ? . . . Canst thou send lightnings, that they may go, and say unto thee, Here we are?" (Job xxxviii.). Of all these wonders, God, was not merely the prima causa; they were the result of His direct action, without any intermediary causes. And it is as absurd to say that the ancient world believed in God, as for a future historian to assert of the nineteenth century that it believed in the effects of electricity. We see them, and so antiquity saw God. If there was any danger, it lay not in the denial of the existence of a God, but in having a wrong belief. Belief in as many gods as there are manifestations in nature, the investing of them with false attributes, the misunderstanding of God's relation to men, lead to immorality. Thus the greater part of the laws and teachings of the Bible are either directed against polytheism, with all its low ideas of God, or rather of gods; or they are directed towards regulating God's relation to men. Man is a servant of God, or His prophet, or even His friend. But this relationship man obtains only by his conduct. Nay, all man's actions are carefully regulated by God, and connected with His holiness. The 19th chapter of Leviticus, which is considered by the Rabbis as the portion of the Law in which the most important articles of the Torah are embodied, is headed, "Ye shall be holy, for I the Lord your own God am holy." And each law therein occurring, even those which concern our relations to each other, is not founded on utilitarian reasons, but is ordained because the opposite of it is an offence to the holiness of God, and profanes His creatures, whom He desired to be as holy as He is. [n. 3]

Thus the whole structure of the Bible is built upon the visible fact of the existence of a God, and upon the belief in the relation of God to men, especially to Israel. In spite of all that has been said to the contrary, the Bible does lay stress upon belief, where belief is required. The unbelievers are rebuked again and again. "For all this they sinned still, and believed not for His wondrous work," complains Asaph (Ps. lxxviii. 32). And belief is praised in such exalted words as, "Thus saith the Lord, I remember thee, the kindness of thy youth, the love of thine espousals, when thou wentest after me in the wilderness, in a land that was not sown" (Jer.ii. 2). The Bible, especially the books of the prophets, consists, in great part, of promises for the future, which the Rabbis justly termed the "Consolations." [n. 4] For our purpose, it is of no great consequence to examine what future the prophets had in view, whether an immediate future or one more remote, at the end of days. At any rate, they inculcated hope and confidence that God would bring to pass a better time. I think that even the most advanced Bible critic -- provided he is not guided by some modern Aryan reasons -- must perceive in such passages as, "The Lord shall reign for ever and ever," "The Lord shall rejoice n his works," and many others, a hope for more than the establishment of the "national Deity among his votaries in Palestine."

We have now to pass over an interval of many centuries, the length of which depends upon the views held is to the date of the close of the canon, and examine what the Rabbis, the representatives of the prophets, thought on this subject. Not that the views of the author of the Wisdom of Solomon, of Philo and Aristobulus, and many others of the Judaeo-Alexandrian school would be uninteresting for us. But somehow their influence on Judaism was only a passing one, and their doctrines never became authoritative in the Synagogue. We must here confine ourselves to those who, even by the testimony of their bitterest enemies, occupied the seat of Moses.

The successors of the prophets had to deal with new circumstances, and accordingly their teachings were adapted to the wants of their times. As the result of manifold foreign influences, the visible fact of the existence of God as manifested in the Bible had been somewhat obscured. Prophecy ceased, and the Holy Spirit which inspired a few chosen ones took its place. Afterwards this influence was reduced to the hearing of a Voice from Heaven, which was audible to still fewer. On the other hand the Rabbis had this advantage that they were not called upon to fight against idolatry as their predecessors the prophets had been. The evil inclination to worship idols was, as the Talmud expresses it allegorically, killed by the Men of the Great Synagogue, or, as we should put it, it was suppressed by the sufferings of the captivity in Babylon. This change of circumstances is marked by the following fact: -- Whilst the prophets mostly considered idolatry as the cause of all sin, the Rabbis show a strong tendency to ascribe sin to a defect in, or a want of, belief on the part of the sinner. They teach that Adam would not have sinned unless he had first denied the "Root of all" (or the main principle), namely, the belief in the Omnipresence of God. Of Cain they say that before murdering his brother he declared: "There is no judgment, there is no judge, there is no world to come, and there is no reward for the just, and no punishment for the wicked." [n. 5]

In another place we read that the commission of a sin in secret is an impertinent attempt by the doer to oust God from the world. But if unbelief is considered as the root of all evil, we may expect that the reverse of it, a perfect faith, would be praised in the most exalted, terms. So we read: Faith is so great that the man who possesses it may hope to become a worthy vessel of the Holy Spirit, or, as we should express it, that he may hope to obtain by this power the highest degree of communion with his Maker. The Patriarch Abraham, notwithstanding all his other virtues, only became "the possessor of both worlds" by the merit of his strong faith. Nay, even the fulfilment of a single law when accompanied by true faith is, according to the Rabbis, sufficient to bring man nigh to God. And the future redemption is also conditional on the degree of faith shown by Israel. [n. 6]

It has often been asked what the Rabbis would have thought of a man who fulfils every commandment of the Torah, but does not believe that this Torah was given by God, or that there exists a God at all. It is indeed very difficult to answer this question with any degree of certainty. In the time of the Rabbis people were still too simple for such a diplomatic religion, and conformity in the modern sense was quite an unknown thing. But from the foregoing remarks it would seem that the Rabbis could not conceive such a monstrosity as atheistic orthodoxy. For, as we have seen, the Rabbis thought that unbelief must needs end in sin, for faith is the origin of all good. Accordingly, in the case just supposed they would have either suspected the man's orthodoxy, or would have denied that his views were really what he professed them to be.

THE MISHNAH - SANHEDRIN AS SOURCE FOR DOGMA

STILL more important than the above cited Agadic passages is one which we are about to quote from the tractate Sanhedrin. This tractate deals with the constitution of the supreme law-court, the examination of the witnesses, the functions of the judges, and the different punishment to be inflicted on the transgressors of the law. After having enumerated various kinds of capital punishment, the Mishnah adds the following words:

"These are (the men) who are excluded from the life to come: He who says there is no resurrection from death; he who says there is no Torah given from heaven, and the Epikurus. [n. 7]

This passage was considered by the Rabbis of the Middle Ages, as well as by modern scholars, the locus classicus for the dogma question. There are many passages in the Rabbinic literature which exclude man from the world to come for this or that sin. But these are more or less of an Agadic (legendary) character, and thus lend themselves to exaggeration and hyperbolic language. They cannot, therefore, be considered as serious legal dicta, or as the general opinion of the Rabbis.

The Mishnah in Sanhedrin, however, has, if only by its position in a legal tractate, a certain Halachic (obligatory) character. And the fact that so early an authority as R. Akiba made additions to it guarantees its high antiquity. The first two sentences of this Mishnah are clear enough. In modern language, and positively speaking, they would represent articles of belief in Resurrection and Revelation. Great difficulty is found in defining what was meant by the word Epicurus. The authorities of the Middle Ages, to whom I shall again have to refer, explain the Epikurus to be a man who denies the belief in reward and punishment; others identify him with one who denies the belief in Providence; while others again consider the Epikurus to be one who denies Tradition. But the parallel passages in which it occurs incline one rather to think that this word cannot be defined by one kind of heresy. It implies rather a frivolous treatment of the words of Scripture or of Tradition. In the case of the latter (Tradition) it is certainly not honest difference of opinion that is condemned; for the Rabbis themselves differed very often from each other, and even Mediaeval authorities, did not feel any compunction about explaining Scripture in variance with the Rabbinic interpretation, and sometimes they even went so far as to declare that the view of this or that great authority was only to be considered as an isolated opinion not deserving particular attention. What they did blame was, as already said, scoffing and impiety. We may thus safely assert that reverence for the teachers of Israel formed the third essential principle of Judaism. [n. 8]

I have still to remark that there occur in the Talmud such passages as "the Jew, even if he has sinned, is still a Jew," or "He who denies idolatry is called a Jew." These and similar passages have been used to prove that Judaism was not a positive religion, but only involved the negation of idolatry. But it has been overlooked that the statements quoted have more a legal than a theological character. The Jew belonged to his nationality even after having committed the greatest sin, just as the Englishman does not cease to be an Englishman -- in regard to treason and the like -- by having committed a heinous crime. But he has certainly acted in a very un-English way, and having outraged the feelings of the whole nation will have to suffer for his misconduct. The Rabbis in a similar manner did not maintain that he who gave up the belief in Revelation and Resurrection, and treated irreverently the teachers of Israel, severed his connection with the Jewish nation, but that, for his crime, he was going to suffer the heaviest punishment. He was to be excluded from the world to come.

Still, important as is the passage quoted from Sanhedrin, it would be erroneous to think that it exhausted the creed of the Rabbis. The liturgy and innumerable passages in the Midrashim show that they ardently clung to the belief in the advent of the Messiah. All their hope was turned to the future redemption and the final establishment of the Kingdom of Heaven on earth. Judaism, stripped of this belief, would have been for them devoid of meaning. The belief in reward and punishment is also repeated again and again in the old Rabbinic literature. A more emphatic declaration of the belief in Providence than is conveyed by the following passages is hardly conceivable. "Everything is foreseen, and free will is given. And the world is judged by grace." Or, "the born are to die, and the dead to revive, and the living to be judged. For to know and to notify, and that it may be known that He (God) is the Framer and He the Creator, and He the Discerner, and He the judge, and He the Witness," etc. [n. 9]

But it must not be forgotten that it was not the habit of the Rabbis to lay down, either for conduct or for doctrine, rules which were commonly known. When they urged the three points stated above there must have been some historical reason for it. Probably these principles were controverted by some heretics. Indeed, the whole tone of the passage cited from Sanhedrin is a protest against certain unbelievers who are threatened with punishment. Other beliefs, not less essential, but less disputed, remain unmentioned, because there was no necessity to assert them.

CARAITE BELIEF

IT was not till a much later time, when the Jews came into closer contact with new philosophical schools, and also new creeds which were more liable than heathenism was to be confused with Judaism, that this necessity was felt. And thus we are led at once to the period when the Jews became acquainted with the teachings of the Mohammedan schools. The Caraites came very early into contact with non-Jewish systems. And so we find that they were also the first to formulate Jewish dogmas in a fixed number, and in a systematic order. It is also possible that their separation from the Tradition, and their early division into little sects among themselves, compelled them to take this step, in order to avoid further sectarianism.

The number of their dogmas amounts to ten. According to Judah Hadasi (150), who would appear to have derived them from his predecessors, their dogmas include the following articles:

1. Creatio ex nihilo;

2. The existence of a Creator, God;

3. This God is an absolute unity as well as incorporeal;

4. Moses and the other prophets were sent by God;

5. God has given to us the Torah, which is true and complete in every respect, not wanting the addition of the so-called Oral Law;

6. The Torah must be studied by every Jew in the original (Hebrew) language;

7. The Holy Temple was a place elected by God for His manifestation;

8. Resurrection of the dead;

9. Punishment and reward after death;

10. The Coming of the Messiah, the son of David.

How far the predecessors of Hadasi were influenced by a certain Joseph Albashir (about 950), of whom there exists a manuscript work, "Rudiments of Faith," I am unable to say. The little we know of him reveals more of his intimacy with Arabic thoughts than of his importance for his sect in particular and for Judaism in general. After Hadasi I shall mention here Elijah Bashazi, a Caraite writer of the end of the fifteenth century. This author, who was much influenced by Maimonides, omits the second and the seventh articles. In order to make up the ten he numbers the belief in the eternity of God as an article, and divides the fourth article into two. In the fifth article Bashazi does not emphasize so strongly the completeness of the Torah as Hadasi, and omits the portion which is directed against Tradition. It is interesting to see the distinction which Bashazi draws between the Pentateuch and the Prophets. While he thinks that the five books of Moses can never be altered, he regards the words of the Prophets as only relating to their contemporaries, and thus subject to changes. As I do not want to anticipate Maimonides' system, I must refrain from giving here the articles laid down by Solomon Troki in the beginning of the eighteenth century. For the articles of Maimonides are copied by this writer with a few slight alterations so as to dress them in a Caraite garb.

I must dismiss the Caraites with these few remarks, my object being chiefly to discuss the dogmas of the Synagogue from which they had separated themselves. Besides, as in everything Caraitic, there is no further development of the question. As Bashazi laid them down, they are still taught by the Caraites of to-day. I return to the Rabbanites. [n.10]

SAADIAH AND THE BEGINNING OF JEWISH DOGMA

AS is well known, Maimonides (1130-1205), was the first Rabbanite who formulated the dogmas of the Synagogue. But there are indications of earlier attempts. R. Saadiah Gaon's (892-942) work, Creeds and Opinions, shows such traces. He says in his preface, "My heart sickens to see that the belief of my co-religionists is impure and that their theological views are confused." The subjects he treats in this book, such as

* creation,
* unity of God,
* resurrection of the dead,
* the future redemption of Israel,
* reward and punishment,

and other kindred theological subjects might thus, perhaps, be considered as the essentials of the creed that the Gaon desired to present in a pure and rational form. R. Hannaneel, of Kairowan, [n. 11] in the first half of the eleventh century, says in one of his commentaries that to deserve eternal life one must believe in four things:

1. in God,

2. in the prophets,

3. in a future world where the just will be rewarded,

4. and in the advent of the Redeemer.

From R. Judah Hallevi's Cusari, written in the beginning of the twelfth century, we might argue that the belief in the election of Israel by God was the cardinal dogma of the author. [n. 12] Abraham Ibn Daud, a contemporary of Maimonides, in his book The High Belief, [n. 13] speaks of rudiments, among which, besides such metaphysical principles as unity, rational conception of God's attributes, etc., the belief in the immutability of the Law, etc., is included. Still, all these works are intended to furnish evidence from philosophy or history for the truth of religion rather than to give a definition of this truth. The latter task was undertaken by Maimonides.

MAIMONIDES AND THE 13 ARTICLES

I refer to the thirteen articles embodied in his first work, The Commentary to the Mishnah. They are appended to the Mishnah in Sanhedrin, with which I dealt above. But though they do not form an independent treatise, Maimonides remarks must not be considered as merely incidental. That Maimonides was quite conscious of the importance of this exposition can be gathered from the concluding words addressed to the reader:

"Know these (words) and repeat them many times, and think them over in the proper way. God knows that thou wouldst be deceiving thyself if thou thinkest thou hast understood them by having read them once or even ten times. Be not, therefore, hasty in perusing them. I have not composed them with out deep study and earnest reflection."

The result of this deep study was that the following Thirteen Articles constitute the creed of Judaism. They are: --

1. The belief in the existence of a Creator;

2. The belief in His Unity;

3. The belief in His Incorporeality;

4. The belief in His Eternity;

5. The belief that all worship and adoration are due to Him alone;

6. The belief in Prophecy;

7. The belief that Moses was the greatest of all Prophets, both before and after him;

8. The belief that the Torah was revealed to Moses on Mount Sinai;

9. The belief in the Immutability of this revealed Torah;

10. The belief that God knows the actions of men;

11. The belief in Reward and Punishment;

12. The belief in the coming of the Messiah;

13. The belief in the Resurrection of the dead.

The impulse given by the great philosopher and still ,greater Jew was eagerly followed by succeeding generations, and Judaism thus came into possession of a dogmatic literature such as it never knew before Maimonides. Maimonides is the centre of this literature, and I shall accordingly speak in the remainder of this essay of Maimonists and Anti-Maimonists. These terms really apply to the great controversy that raged round Maimonides Guide of the Perplexed, but I shall, chiefly for brevity's sake, employ them in these pages in a restricted sense to refer to the dispute concerning the Thirteen Articles.

Among the Maimonists we may probably include the great majority of Jews, who accepted the Thirteen Articles without further question. Maimonides must indeed have filled up a great gap in Jewish theology, a gap, moreover, the existence of which was very generally perceived. A century had hardly elapsed before the Thirteen Articles had become a theme for the poets of the Synagogue. And almost every country where Jews lived can show a poem or a prayer founded on these Articles. R. Jacob Molin (1420) of Germany speaks of metrical and rhymed songs in the German language, the burden of which was the Thirteen Articles, and which were read by the common people with great devotion. The numerous commentaries and homilies written on the same topic would form a small library in themselves. [n. 14] But on the other hand it must not be denied that the Anti-Maimonists, that is to say those Jewish writers who did not agree with the creed formulated by Maimonides, or agreed only in part with him, form also a very strong and respectable minority. They deserve our attention the more as it is their works which brought life into the subject and deepened it. It is not by a perpetual Amen to every utterance of a great authority that truth or literature gains anything.

THE ANTI-MAIMONISTS

THE Anti-Maimonists can be divided into two classes. The one class categorically denies that Judaism has dogmas. I shall have occasion to touch on this view when I come to speak of Abarbanel. Here I pass at once to the second class of Anti-Maimonists. This consists of those who agree with Maimonides as to the existence of dogmas in Judaism, but who differ from him as to what these dogmas are, or who give a different enumeration of them.

As the first of these Anti-Maimonists we may regard Nachmanides, who, in his famous Sermon in the Presence of the King, speaks of three fundamental principles:

* Creation (that is, non-eternity of matter),
* Omniscience of God, and
* Providence.

Next comes R. Abba Mari ben Moses, of Montpellier. He wrote at the beginning of the fourteenth century, and is famous in Jewish history for his zeal against the study of philosophy. We possess a small pamphlet by him dealing with our subject, and it forms a kind of prologue to his collection of controversial letters against the rationalists of his time. [n. 15] He lays down three articles as the fundamental teachings of Religion:

1. Metaphysical: The existence of God, including His Unity and Incorporeality;

2. Mosaic: Creatio ex nihilo by God -- a consequence of this principle is the belief that God is capable of altering the laws of nature at His pleasure;

3. Ethical: Special Providence -- i.e., God knows all our actions in all their details.

Abba Mari does not mention Maimonides' Thirteen Articles. But it would be false to conclude that he rejected the belief in the coming of the Messiah, or any other article of Maimonides. The whole tone and tendency of this pamphlet is polemical, and it is therefore probable that he only urged those points which were either doubted or explained in an unorthodox way by the sceptics of his time.

Another scholar, of Provence, who wrote but twenty years later than Abba Mari -- R. David ben Samuel d'Estella (1320) -- speaks of the seven pillars of religion. They are:

* Revelation,
* Providence,
* Reward and Punishment,
* the Coming of the Messiah,
* Resurrection of the Dead,
* Creatio ex nihilo, and
* Free Will. [n. 16]

Of authors living, in other countries, I have to mention here R. Shemariah, of Crete, who flourished at about the same time as R. David d'Estella, and is known from his efforts to reconcile the Caraites with the Rabbanites. This author wrote a book for the purpose of furnishing Jewish students with evidence for what he considered the five fundamental teachings of Judaism, viz.:

1. The Existence of God;

2. The Incorporeality of God;

3. His Absolute Unity;

4. That God created heaven and earth;

5. That God created the world after His will 5106 years ago -- 5106 (1346 A.C.), being the year in which Shemariah wrote these words. [n. 17]

In Portugal, at about the same time, we find R. David ben Yom-Tob Bilia adding to the articles of Maimonides thirteen of his own, which he calls the "Fundamentals of the Thinking Man." Five of these articles relate to the functions of the human soul, that, according to him, emanated from God, and to the way in which this divine soul receives its punishment and reward. The other eight articles are as follows:

1. The belief in the existence of spiritual beings -- angels;

2. Creatio ex nihilo,

3. The belief in the existence of another world, and that this other world is only a spiritual one;

4. The Torah is above philosophy;

5. The Torah has an outward (literal) meaning and an inward (allegorical) meaning;

6. The text of the Torah is not subject to any emendation;

7. The reward of a good action is the good work itself, and the doer must not expect any other reward;

8. It is only by the "commands relating to the heart," for instance, the belief in one eternal God, the loving and fearing Him, and not through good actions, that man attains the highest degree of perfection. [n. 18]

Perhaps it would be suitable to mention here another contemporaneous writer, who also enumerates twenty-six articles. The name of this writer is unknown, and his articles are only gathered from quotations by later authors. It would seem from these quotations that the articles of this unknown author consisted mostly of statements emphasising the belief in the attributes of God: as, His Eternity, His Wisdom and Omnipotence, and the like. [n.19]

More important for our subject are the productions of the fifteenth century, especially those of Spanish authors. The fifteen articles of R. Lipman Muhlhausen, in the preface to his well-known Book of Victory [n. 20] (1410), differ but slightly from those of Maimonides. In accordance with the anti-Christian tendency of his polemical book, he lays more stress on the two articles of Unity and Incorporeality, and makes of them four. We can therefore dismiss him with this short remark, and pass at once to the Spanish Rabbis.

CHASDAI IBN CRESCAS

THE first of these is R. Chasdai Ibn Crescas, who composed his famous treatise, The Light of God, about 1405. Chasdai's book is well known for its attacks on Aristotle, and also for its influence on Spinoza. But Chasdai deals also with Maimonides' Thirteen Articles, to which he was very strongly opposed. Already in his preface he attacks Maimonides for speaking, in his Book of the Commandments, of the belief in the existence of God as an "affirmative precept." Chasdai thinks it absurd; for every commandment must be dictated by some authority, but on whose authority can we dictate the acceptance of this authority? His general objection to the Thirteen Articles is that Maimonides confounded dogmas or fundamental beliefs of Judaism, without which Judaism is inconceivable, with beliefs or doctrines which Judaism inculcates, but the denial of which, though involving a strong heresy, does not make Judaism impossible. He maintains that if Maimonides meant only to count fundamental teachings, there are not more than seven; but that if he intended also to include doctrines, he ought to have enumerated sixteen. As beliefs of the first class -- namely, fundamental beliefs -- he considers the following articles:

1. God's knowledge of our actions;

2. Providence;

3. God's omnipotence -- even to act against the laws of nature;

4. Prophecy;

5. Free will;

6. The aim of the Torah is to make man long after the closest communion with God.

The belief in the existence of God, Chasdai thinks, is an axiom with which every religion must begin, and he is therefore uncertain whether to include it as a dogma or not. As to the doctrines which every Jew is bound to believe, but without which Judaism is not impossible, Chasdai divides them into two sections: (a)

1. Creatio ex nihilo;

2. Immortality of the soul;

3. Reward and Punishment;

4. Resurrection of the dead;

5. Immutability of the Torah;

6. Superiority of the prophecy of Moses;

7. That the High Priest received from God the instructions sought for, when he put his questions through the medium of the Urim and Thummim;

8. The coming of the Messiah.

(b) Doctrines which are expressed by certain religious ceremonies, and on belief in which these ceremonies are conditioned:

1. The belief in the efficacy of prayer as well as in the power of the benediction of the priests to convey to us the blessing of God;

2. God is merciful to the penitent;

3. Certain days in the year -- for instance, the Day of Atonement -- are especially qualified to bring us near to God, if we keep them in the way we are commanded.

That Chasdai is a little arbitrary in the choice of his "doctrines," I need hardly say. Indeed, Chasdai's importance for the dogma-question consists more in his critical suggestions than in his positive results. He was, as we have seen, the first to make the distinction between fundamental teachings which form the basis of Judaism, and those other simple Jewish doctrines without which Judaism is not impossible. Very daring is his remark, when proving that Reward and Punishment, Immortality of the soul, and Resurrection of the dead must not be considered as the basis of Judaism, since the highest ideal of religion is to serve God without any hope of reward. Even more daring are his words concerning the Immutability of the Law. He says: "Some have argued that, since God is perfection, so must also His law be perfect, and thus unsusceptible of improvement." But he does not think this argument conclusive, though the fact in itself (the Immutability of the Law) is true. For one might answer that this perfection of the Torah could only be in accordance with the intelligence of those for whom it was meant; but as soon as the recipients of the Torah have advanced to a higher state of perfection, the Torah must also be altered to suit their advanced intelligence. A pupil of Chasdai illustrates the words of his master by a medical parallel. The physician has to adapt his medicaments to the various stages through which his patient has to pass. That he changes his prescription does not, however, imply that his medical knowledge is imperfect, or that his earlier remedies were ignorantly chosen; the varying condition of the invalid was the cause of the variation in the doctor's treatment. Similarly, were not the Immutability of the Torah a "doctrine," one might maintain that the perfection of the Torah would not be inconsistent with the assumption that it was susceptible of modification, in accordance with our changing and progressive circumstances. But all these arguments are purely of a theoretic character; for, practically, every Jew, according to Chasdai, has to accept all these beliefs) whether he terms them fundamental teachings or only Jewish doctrines. [n. 21]

Some years later, though he finished his work in the same year as Chasdai, R. Simeon Duran (1366-1444,) a younger contemporary of the former, made his researches on dogmas. His studies on this subject form a kind of introduction to his commentary on Job, which he finished in the year 1405. Duran is not so strongly opposed to the Thirteen Articles as Chasdai, or as another "thinker of our people," who thought them an arbitrary imitation of the thirteen attributes of God. Duran tries to justify Maimonides; but nevertheless he agrees with "earlier authorities," who formulated the Jewish creed in Three Articles -- The Existence of God, Revelation, and Reward and Punishment -- under which Duran thinks the Thirteen Articles of Maimonides may be easily classed. Most interesting are his remarks concerning the validity of dogmas. He tells us that only those are to be considered as heretics who abide by their own opinions, though they know that they are contradictory to the views of the Torah. Those who accept the fundamental teachings of Judaism, but are led by their deep studies and earnest reflection to differ in details from the opinions current among their co-religionists, and explain certain passages in the Scripture in their own way, must by no means be considered as heretics. We must, therefore, Duran proceeds to say, not blame such men as Maimonides, who gave an allegorical interpretation to certain passages in the Bible about miracles, or R. Levi ben Gershom, who followed certain un-Jewish views in relation to the belief in Creatio ex nihilo. Only the views are condemnable, not those who cherish them. God forbid, says Duran, that such a thing should happen in Israel as to condemn honest inquirers on account of their differing opinions. It would be interesting to know of how many divines as tolerant as this persecuted Jew the fifteenth century can boast. [n. 21]

ALBO

WE can now pass to a more popular but less original writer on our theme. I refer to R. Joseph Albo, the author of the Roots, [n. 23] who was the pupil of Chasdai, a younger contemporary of Duran, and wrote at a much later period than these authors. Graetz has justly denied him much originality. The chief merit of Albo consists in popularising other people's thoughts, though he does not always take care to mention their names. And the student who is a little familiar with the contents of the Roots will easily find that Albo has taken his best ideas either from Chasdai or from Duran. As it is of little consequence to us whether an article of faith is called "stem," or "root," or "branch," there is scarcely anything fresh left to quote in the name of Albo. The late Dr. Low, of Szegedin, was indeed right, when he answered an adversary who challenged him -- "Who would dare to declare me a heretic as long as I confess the Three Articles laid down by Albo?" with the words "Albo himself." For, after all the subtle distinctions Albo makes between different classes of dogmas, he declares that every one who denies even the immutability of the Law or the coming of the Messiah, which are, according to him, articles of minor importance, is a heretic who will be excluded from the world to come. But there is one point in his book which is worth noticing. It was suggested to him by Maimonides, indeed; still Albo has the merit of having emphasised it as it deserves. Among the articles which he calls "branches" Albo counts the belief that the perfection of man, which leads to eternal life, can be obtained by the fulfilling of one commandment. But this command must, as Maimonides points out, be done without any worldly regard, and only for the love of God. When one considers how many platitudes are repeated year by year by certain theologians on the subject of Jewish legalism, we cannot lay enough stress on this article of Albo, and we ought to make it better known than it has hitherto been. [n. 24]

Though I cannot enter here into the enumeration of the Maimonists, I must not leave unmentioned the name of R. Nissim ben Moses of Marseilles, the first great Maimonist, who flourished about the end of the thirteenth century, and was considered as one of the most enlightened thinkers of his age. [n. 25] Another great Maimonist deserving special attention is R. Abraham ben Shem-Tob Bibago, who may perhaps be regarded as the most prominent among those who undertook to defend Maimonides against the attacks of Chasdai and others. Bibago wrote The Path of Belief [n.26] in the second half of the fifteenth century, and was, as Dr. Steinschneider aptly describes him, a Denkglaubiger. But, above all, he was a believing Jew. When he was once asked, at the table of King John II., of Aragon, by a Christian scholar, "Are you the Jewish philosopher?" he answered, "I am a Jew who believes in the Law given to us by our teacher Moses, though I have studied philosophy." Bibago was such a devoted admirer of Maimonides that he could not tolerate any opposition to him. He speaks in one passage of the prudent people of his time who, in desiring to be looked upon as orthodox by the great mob, calumniated the Teacher (Maimonides), and depreciated his merits. Bibago's book is very interesting, especially in its controversial parts; but in respect to dogmas he is, as already said, a Maimonist, and does not contribute any new point on our subject.

To return to the Anti-Maimonists of the second half of the fifteenth century. As such may be considered R. Isaac Aramah, who speaks of three foundations of religion:

* Creatio ex nihilo,
* Revelation (?),
* and the belief in a world to come. [n. 27]

Next to be mentioned is R. Joseph Jabez, who also accepts only three articles:

* Creatio ex nihilo,
* Individual Providence, and
* the Unity of God. [n. 22]

Under these three heads he tries to classify the Thirteen Articles of Maimonides.

ABARBANEL

THE last Spanish writer on our subject is R. Isaac Abarbanel. His treatise on the subject is known under the title Top of Amanah [n. 29] and was finished in the year 1495. The greatest part of this treatise forms a defence of Maimonides, many points in which are taken from Bibago. But, in spite of this fact, Abarbanel must not be considered a Maimonist. It is only a feeling of piety towards Maimonides, or perhaps rather a fondness for argument, that made him defend Maimonides against Chasdai and others. His own view is that it is a mistake to formulate dogmas of Judaism, since every word in the Torah has to be considered as a dogma for itself. It was only, says Abarbanel, by following the example of non-Jewish scholars that Maimonides and others were induced to lay down dogmas. The non-Jewish philosophers are in the habit of accepting in every science certain indisputable axioms from which they deduce the propositions which are less evident. The Jewish philosophers in a similar way sought for first principles in religion from which the whole of the Torah ought to be considered as a deduction. But, thinks Abarbanel, the Torah as a revealed code is under no necessity of deducing things from each other, for all the commandments came from the same divine authority, and, therefore, are alike evident, and have the same certainty. On this and similar grounds Abarbanel refused to acccept dogmatic articles for Judaism, and he this became the head of the school that forms a class by itself among the anti-Maimonists to which many of the great Cabbalists belong. But it is idle talk to cite this school in aid of the modern theory that Judaism has no dogmas. As we have seen, it was rather an embarras de riches that prevented Abarbanel from accepting the Thirteen Articles of Maimonides. To him and to the Cabbalists the Torah consists of at least 613 Articles.

Abarbanel wrote his book with which we have just dealt, at Naples. And it is Italy to which, after the expulsion of the Jews from Spain, we have to look chiefly for religious speculation. But the philosophers of Italy are still less independent of Maimonides than their predecessor in Spain. Thus we find that R. David Messer Leon, R. David Vital, and others were Maimonists.

DELMEDIGO

EVEN the otherwise refined and original thinker, R. Elijah Delmedigo (who died about the end of the fifteenth century) becomes almost impolite when he speaks of the adversaries of Maimonides in respect to dogmas. "It was only," he says, "the would-be philosopher that dared to question the articles of Maimonides. Our people have always the bad habit of thinking themselves competent to attack the greatest authorities as soon as they have got some knowledge of the subject. Genuine thinkers, however, attach very little importance to their objections." [n. 30]

Indeed, it seems as if the energetic protests of Delmedigo scared away the Anti-Maimonists for more than a century. Even in the following seventeenth century we have to notice only two Anti-Maimonists. The one is R. Tobijah, the Priest (1652), who was of Polish descent, studied in Italy, and lived as a medical man in France. He seems to refuse to accept the belief in the Immutability of the Torah, and in the coming of the Messiah, as fundamental teachings of Judaism. [n. 31] The other, at the end of the seventeenth century (1695), is R. Abraham Chayim Viterbo, of Italy. He accepts only six articles:

1. Existence of God;

2. Unity;

3. Incorporeality;

4. That God was revealed to Moses on Mount Sinai, and that the prophecy of Moses is true;

5. Revelation (including the historical parts of the Torah);

6. Reward and Punishment.

As to the other articles of Maimonides, Viterbo, in opposition to other half-hearted Anti-Maimonists, declares that the man who denies them is not to be considered as a heretic ; though he ought to believe them. [n. 32]

I have now arrived at the limit I set to myself at the beginning of this essay. For, between the times of Viterbo and those of Mendelssohn, there is hardly to be found any serious opposition to Maimonides worth noticing here. Still I must mention the name of R. Saul Berlin (died 1794); there is much in his opinions on dogmas which will help us the better to understand the Thirteen Articles of Maimonides. As the reader has seen, I have refrained so far from reproducing here the apologies which were made by many Maimonists in behalf of the Thirteen Articles. For, after all their elaborate pleas, none of them was able to clear Maimonides of the charge of having confounded dogmas or fundamental teachings with doctrines. It is also true that the Fifth Article -- that prayer and worship must only be offered to God -- cannot be considered even as a doctrine, but as a simple precept. And there are other difficulties which all the distinctions of the Maimonists will never be able to solve. The only possible justification is, I think, that suggested by a remark of R. Saul. This author, who was himself -- like his friend and older contemporary Mendelssohn -- a strong Anti-Maimonist, among other remarks, maintains that dogmas must never be laid down but with regard to the necessities of the time. [n. 33]

Now R. Saul certainly did not doubt that Judaism is based on eternal truths which can in no way be shaken by new modes of thinking or changed circumstances. What he meant was that there are in every age certain beliefs which ought to be asserted more emphatically than others, without regard to their theological or rather logical importance. It is by this maxim that we shall be able to explain the articles of Maimonides. He asserted them, because they were necessary for his time.

We know, for instance, from a letter of his son and from other contemporaries, that it was just at his time that the belief in the incorporeality of God was, in the opinion of Maimonides, a little relaxed. Maimonides, who thought such low notions of the Deity dangerous to Judaism, therefore laid down an article against them. He tells us in his Guide that it was far from him to condemn any one who was not able to demonstrate the Incorporeality of God, but he stigmatised as a heretic one who refused to believe it. This position might be paralleled by that of a modern astronomer who, while considering it unreasonable to expect a mathematical demonstration of the movements of the earth from an ordinary unscientific man, would yet regard the person who refused to believe in such movements as an ignorant faddist.

Again, Maimonides undoubtedly knew that there may be found in the Talmud -- that bottomless sea with its innumerable undercurrents -- passages that are not quite in harmony with his articles; for instance, the well-known dictum of R. Hillel, who said, there is no Messiah for Israel -- a passage which has already been quoted ad nauseam by every opponent of Maimonides from the earliest times down to the year of grace 1896. Maimonides was well aware of the existence of this and similar passages. But, being deeply convinced of the necessity of the belief in a future redemption of Israel -- in opposition to other creeds which claim this redemption exclusively for their own adherents -- Maimonides simply ignored the saying of R. Hillel, as an isolated opinion which contradicts all the consciousness and traditions of the Jew as expressed in thousands of other passages, and especially in the liturgy. Most interesting is Maimonides' view about such isolated opinions in a letter to the wise men of Marseilles. He deals there with the question of free will and other theological subjects. After having stated his own view he goes on to say:

"I know that it is possible to find in the Talmud or in the Midrash this or that saying in contradiction to the views you have heard from me. But you must not be troubled by them. One must not refuse to accept a doctrine, the truth of which has been proved, on account of its being in opposition to some isolated opinion held by this or that great authority. Is it not possible that he overlooked some important considerations when he uttered this strange opinion ? It is also possible that his words must not be taken literally, and have to be explained in an allegorical way. We can also think that his words were only to be applied with regard to certain circumstances of his time, but never intended as permanent truths. . . . No man must surrender his private judgment. The eyes are not directed backwards but forwards."

In another place Maimonides calls the suppression of one's own opinions for the reason of their being irreconcilable with the isolated views of some great authority -- a moral suicide.

By such motives Maimonides was guided when he left certain views hazarded in the Rabbinic literature unheeded, and followed what we may perhaps call the religious instinct, trusting to his own conscience. We may again be certain that Maimonides was clear-headed enough to see that the words of the Torah: "And there arose no prophet since in Israel like unto Moses" (Deut. xxxiv. 10), were as little intended to imply a doctrine as the passage relating to the king Josiah, "And like unto him was there no king before him that turned to the Lord with all his heart . . . neither after him arose there any like him" (2 Kings xxiii. 25). And none would think of declaring the man a heretic who should believe another king to be as pious as Josiah. But living among followers of the "imitating creeds" (as he calls Christianity and Mohammedism), who claimed that their religion had superseded the law of Moses, Maimonides, consciously or unconsciously, felt himself compelled to assert the superiority of the prophecy of Moses. And so we may guess that every article of Maimonides which seems to offer difficulties to us contains an assertion of some relaxed belief, or a protest against the pretensions of other creeds, though we are not always able to discover the exact necessity for them. On the other hand, Maimonides did not assert the belief in free will, for which he argued so earnestly in his Guide. The common "man," with his simple unspeculative mind, for whom these Thirteen Articles were intended, "never dreamed that the will was not free," and there was no necessity of impressing on his mind things which he had never doubted. [n. 34]

So much about Maimonides. As to the Anti-Maimonists, it could hardly escape the reader that in some of the quoted systems the difference from the view of Maimonides is only a logical one, not a theological. Of some authors again, especially those of the thirteenth and fourteenth centuries, it is not at all certain whether they intended to oppose Maimonides. Others again, as for instance R. Abba Mari, R. Lipman, and R. Joseph Jabez, acted on the same principle as Maimonides, urging only those teachings of Judaism which they thought endangered. One could now, indeed, animated by the praiseworthy examples given to us by Maimonides, also propose some articles of faith which are suggested to us by the necessities of our own time.

One might, for instance, insert the article, "I believe that Judaism is, in the first instance, a divine religion, not a mere complex of racial peculiarities and tribal customs." One might again propose an article to the effect that Judaism is a proselytising religion, having the mission to bring about God's kingdom on earth, and to include in that kingdom all mankind. One might also submit for consideration whether, it would not be advisable to urge a little more the principle that religion means chiefly a Weltanschauung and worship of God by means of holiness both in thought and in action. One would even not object to accept the article laid down by R. Saul, that we have to look upon ourselves as sinners. Morbid as such a belief may be, it would, if properly impressed on our mind, have perhaps the wholesome effect of cooling down a little our self importance and our mutual admiration that makes all progress among us almost impossible.

But it was not my purpose to ventilate here the question whether Maimonides' articles are sufficient for us, or whether we ought not to add new ones to them. Nor do I attempt to decide what system we ought to prefer for recitation in the Synagogue -- that of Maimonides or that of Chasdai, or of any other writer. I do not think that such a recital is of much use. My object in this sketch has been rather to make the reader think about Judaism, by proving that it regulates not only our actions, but also our thoughts. We usually urge that in Judaism religion means life; but we forget that a life without guiding principles and thoughts is a Life not worth living. At least it was so considered by the greatest Jewish thinkers, and hence their efforts to formulate the creed of Judaism, so that men should not only be able to do the right thing, but also to think the right thing. Whether they succeeded in their attempts towards formulating the creed of Judaism or not will always remain a question. This concerns the logician more than the theologian.

But surely Maimonides and his successors did succeed in having a religion depending directly on God, with the most ideal and lofty aspirations for the future; whilst the Judaism of a great part of our modern theologians reminds one very much of the words with which the author of Marius the Epicurean characterises the Roman religion in the days of her decline: a religion which had been always something to be done rather than something to be thought, or believed, or loved.

Political economy, hygiene, statistics, are very fine things. But no sane man would for them make those sacrifices which Judaism requires from us. It is only for God's sake, to fulfil His commands and to accomplish His purpose, that religion becomes worth living and dying for. And this can only be possible with a religion which possesses dogmas.

It is true that every great religion is "a concentration of many ideas and ideals," which make this religion able to adapt itself to various modes of thinking and living. But there must always be a point round which all these ideas concentrate themselves. This centre is Dogma.

www.ingramcontent.com/pod-product-compliance
Lightning Source LLC
Chambersburg PA
CBHW040747020526
44118CB00040B/2701